THE BOOK OF TREES

SAINT JULIAN PRESS

POETRY

Praise for THE BOOK OF TREES

The outcome of spiritual contemplation is not beauty, certainly not worldly beauty, neither is the outcome worldly comfort. And yet our contemplation occurs necessarily in the world and is of the world. This is the paradox one must accept if the spiritual life is to be deepened and extended. As this absorbing book makes clear, we have nature and language to house this paradox, indeed, to give it life, that we may grasp it and live with it. An ancient world is fully alive in these poems, tended by a devoted hand. This is a rich and satisfying book, a transport and a safe return at once. One may conclude that serious contemplation is never solitary—it is, like art, an act of fellowship.

Maurice Manning, finalist for the Pulitzer Prize:
author of *The Gone and the Going Away* (2013),
and *One Man's Dark* (2016).

Both elegiac and radical, Sean M. Conrey's fascinating *The Book of Trees* imagines and recreates the voice of Saint Columba, the 6th century Irish priest and scholar once known as Columcille. Melding ekphrasis (inspired by the Ogham alphabet) and dramatic monologue, Conrey's thickly intertextual poems deftly find the seam between the Catholic and Druidic legacies of Ireland. Through the voice of one who partook in the erasure of pagan wisdom, Conrey works to recover what we might have lost in the triumph of Catholicism, to discover what Fanny Howe calls the "God behind God."

Philip Metres, author of *Sand Opera*

In the opening lines of "Willow," a poem in Sean M. Conrey's latest, *The Book of Trees*, Saint Columba imagines Christ in a rainless desert, a landscape he knows only through books. The poem ends with a vignette about a monk who perches on Columba's shoulders to repair a thatched roof in the midst of a downpour—"I'll admit, it's a constant struggle to love/the mud on my shoulders where he stood." With the cadence of prayer, Conrey's poems conjure the wisdom of a land that hasn't "forgot to speak for itself" at the very moment when that wisdom begins to be forgotten. A briny and true collection.

Jennifer Glancy, Professor of Religious Studies at Le Moyne College and author of *Corporal Knowledge: Early Christian Bodies*

In Sean M. Conrey's stunning second book of poems, he explores the voice of Saint Columba, the Irish missionary who, among other achievements, brought Christianity to Scotland and founded the abbey at Iona. Using the ogham script as his organizing principle, and starting from histories, scripture, original texts, and the Gnostic gospels, Conrey's chiseled lines give us stories of both the physical and spiritual labors of Columba and his fellow monks— men who might spend a hungry winter carving buttons from the bones of their dead livestock, or who might launch themselves into the sea, for penance, aboard a boat with no oars. This is not a romantic tale of glory, however. In Conrey's retelling, Columba recognizes that it is "A danger of history, / to purify the saints and mistake / Christ's forgiveness / for never having sinned." Doubt is a frequent guest to this narrator, who laments that he sees "far, but not far enough," and who recognizes frequently the impact his men make upon the natural world: "The wind is warming," Columba muses in one poem, "Have mercy on those who made it so." *The Book of Trees* is full of striking moments such as this, in which the current and ancient seem nearly contemporaneous, and in which we can, through the struggles of a man fifteen centuries past, perhaps recognize a brother.

Philip Memmer, author of
The Storehouses of the Snow: Psalms, Parables, and Dreams

THE BOOK
OF TREES

Poems By

Sean M. Conrey

SAINT JULIAN PRESS
HOUSTON

Published by
SAINT JULIAN PRESS, Inc.
2053 Cortlandt, Suite 200
Houston, Texas 77008

www.saintjulianpress.com

ISBN-13: 978-0-9986404-3-3
ISBN: 0-9986404-3-3
Library of Congress Control Number: 2017958355

Cover Art Credit: Emily Bender-Murphy
Author Photo Credit: Stephen Davies

FOREWORD

❖

"Don't look down," I instructed my brother. I had once seen our cat clamor only half as high and freeze in the same way. *Left foot, down, a little more,* but his bare foot was hesitant. The air had changed. It wasn't there to hold him. The wordless language of childhood—his Morse code of whimpering and sniveling sent me sprinting indoors, calling for my mom. I read and reread the page of my mom's face, and though she was calm, I could see her shock. She deciphered a way down, puzzling out a path he could not see below him, what to grab and how, where to reach his foot and where to plant it. Her calm voice led him out of wild fear. Finally, he was in the forked arms of his favorite branch and shaky with relief. Only then did he wail. My mom reached up, matter-of-fact. She'd always known he'd come to earth.

It seems right that after rereading Sean M. Conrey's *The Book of Trees*, this memory surfaced. Clearly, this is a poet who has climbed the many branched uncertainties and ferocious joys of a life of faith, much like the complex speaker of his poems, Saint Columba.

Sean and I were MFA students together, 18 years ago, workshopping poems and studying craft. I was a fiction writer, but I had come into fiction through the window of poetry. His mind was a wondrous web, making connections, gathering in a bounty of sources. Honestly, often I couldn't keep up. He was always reading. Always writing. Always ready to talk until the wee hours about both, bringing in world history, popular culture, geography, geology, song lyrics, and art. He soon became one of my favorite people, one of the people I looked to, learned from, and respected as a writer. All of these years later, he is one of the rare people I still share my poetry with, one of the rare people who knows me, trusted even in the moments when, too high up, I am unable to imagine a way to safety. His voice has brought me back to earth.

He knows how complicated faith is. And yet, he has reminded me, as a friend and as a poet, to trust. Trust that I have the strength that life and love require.

What a rich and brilliant harvest awaits the reader in *The Book of Trees*. Historically layered, richly imagined, Sean does what many writers dream of but are unable to enact—he brings the past alive with the fertile loam of his craft, and makes us also consider the *now*. And yet, these considerations only occur after we exit the exquisite world and time and stories of these poems, after we've already been changed by them. Sean walks the tightrope he addresses so eloquently in the afterword, forcing us to acknowledge and "work *through* that violence" of Columba's time and texts, and our own—our own individual worlds and the one we all share. He does this by exploring the living language of the ogham script, known to druids and a handful of early Irish Christians, a script which, through the act of writing, becomes a forest of letters to climb to consider and become closer to the Divine.

Yet within the order of these poems is the wilderness of being human, longing for God, journeying toward delight and being fully alive, accepting small and hugely incomprehensible deaths, knowingly turning from, and then willingly turning toward, God. In Columba, we see our hunger to be living prayer, a desire to open our hearts, "alive and delighted," to wake and "begin anew this morning." Through Columba, we are reminded to see God in all things, even in the suffering we must endure ("Endure, you say across the span, /midway now from winter to spring, /make way as a road makes way"). Climbing through these poems, I want to believe in Christ, "To think of such a man as could die/ to show us all dying is always remade, / knotted through the soil's dark text/ till at last we come again, green, anew…." And yet, I know the dark rooms of Columba's heart too. I find myself there when he reflects on living in a faith community, working to fix the leak in a thatched roof. "Next day, a monk stands on my shoulders, / skitters to fix it in a steady rain, smiling. /I'll admit, it's a constant struggle to love/ the mud on my shoulders where he stood."

This collection of poems arrived at a time when I felt untethered, parched, and feverishly uncertain about what it meant to love and serve God and others, and what it meant to love myself. These poems speak to this condition, begging to be read aloud:

> Faith is the earth in which we take root,
> hope the water through which we are nourished,
> love the wind through which we aspire,
> knowledge the light through which we ripen.
> Use these tools that we may eat.

Through these poems, Sean offers us a layered communion. His work nourishes and sustains, reminding us that there is always a path, and "we must find a way through, / though as we're beginning, / an end grows near."

My own father has instructed me to sprinkle his ashes around the base of a massive oak on his father's farm. "There's no way of knowing when," he said, tapping his pipe against the trunk hard enough to clear the ash. "Listen," my daughter said as the wind set the leaves into chorus, lifting her face and her arms up. We stood and listened, our faces dappled by the lace of sunlight cast through the canopy.

We, all of us, will feed the tree.

Barbara C. Lawhorn
Western Illinois University
Department of English

FOR MIRA AND EMILY

C O N T E N T S

SAINT COLUMBA'S PSALM ... 1

FIRST AICME

    ⊢ BIRCH ... 5

    ⊨ ROWAN ... 7

    ⊫ ALDER ... 9

    ⊨ WILLOW ... 11

    ⊫ ASH ... 13

SECOND AICME

    ⊣ HAWTHORN ... 17

    ⊩ OAK ... 18

    ≡ HOLLY ... 19

    ≣ HAZEL ... 21

    ≣APPLE ... 23

THIRD AICME

    ⊥ VINE ... 27

    ⊯ IVY ... 28

    ≢ BROOM ... 30

    ≣ BLACKTHORN ... 32

    ≣ ELDER ... 33

FOURTH AICME

✛ SILVER FIR ... 37

✚ GORSE ... 39

╪ HEATHER ... 40

╪ ASPEN ... 41

╪ YEW ... 44

NOTES ... 47

AFTERWORD ... 59

THE BOOK OF TREES

On an island hill's rain-clean stone,
alive and delighted
that I may stare across the quiet sea.

That I may attend to heavy waves,
lines of light, the endless music
given to the Father.

That to the eye creation alights,
bright sand, a wave's white edge,
strange birds, new and fine voices.

That below, where waves whisper
on rocks, the sea
is a voice crying at the graveside.

That a knot of birds above the water
scatters when a whale crests –
I am fully alive.

That I may stare across the flood
and confess my name in private –
"He who turned his back on Ireland."

~*~

FIRST AICME

┝

BIRCH

Glory be to the Father,
gentle or severe, the light behind the sun,
and to the Son Himself,
whose voice pulls seeds toward the light,
and to the Holy Spirit,
who holds the two in three, ever-shining –
As it was in the beginning, is now,
and ever shall be, world without end –

And I begin, born anew this morning,
every morning the same,
with the sun, bright or clouded-gray.
This frigid day of Kentigern
I take again a pen in hand
to cast old shadows on the page
in Jerome's vulgar letters,
though this morning I have in mind
the stone-hewn older shapes.

It's right to refresh the memory,
so let us recall the beginning,
the birch, the river Barrow,
the color *bán*, the church at Bangor,
the Bruden fortress, the art of betterment,
Saint Brendan, a loaf of bread, and back
to the birch, white and straight,
the first of twenty.

Through these branches let the pages
of the gospel blow
like leaves across the earth's face,
through valleys and alluvia,
near rivers, be they Barrow,
Liffey, or Foyle,
Betsie, Licking, or Flushing –

At the river's edge let us begin,
past birch for a start
through the traveler's tree, rowan,
to alder, from root to leaf a gift —
this forest a litany, a letter
to read as the trumpets blare —
we must find a way through,
though as we're beginning,
an end grows near.

⊨

ROWAN

I was a word in letters,
a book in origin,
a night bird staring
at Fursey's four fires,
on knees praying
amid standing stones
writ with crosses
at their tops, alone
in a rain with a turf fire
near to warm me.

We were stones
split from the mountain,
stones set in a wall,
the wall knocked apart
by the army at Cúl Dreimhne,
encircled in fog
at Benbulben's foot,
where the old gods
still held sway.

It's true, friends,
His voice was thin
when we twelve set out,
silent, broken, barely men,
in a curragh, in a trough
between waves,
rocks washed in brine,
we came to Iona
in a small drizzle.

The Lord replied
in language and land,
thus was I scattered,
and thus I learned
I'd been a black road
in green fields,
a felled oak
damming a cold stream,
but I'd not resist
His current again.

⊨ ALDER

Bring the wind through your berries,
a crow in the branches, a necklace in its beak,
a fallow field washed bare by rain,
Orion's belt, the new moon waxing.

Brigid sing a song for your mother,
tethered to the king, your father,
your brothers out playing at swords
while we pray, 'Hail Mary of the Gael,'
born not of a virgin, but a broken slave girl,
we love you full well, sister.

You're a linen-clad flower in Connacht,
a warm face against the shadows of the fire,
a weeping child for seven days lost,
a crone gathering wood in midwinter,
an earth-brown blanket on the dead,
the wood smoldering in the oven,
soft within and hard without, the bread.

In you we endure since the solstice,
walk the steps to Kildare's grove,
pull the last empty nets from the Liffey,
break the frozen skin from the pail.

Endure, you say across the span,
midway now from winter to spring,
make way as a road makes way.

Through you we move as the wind
through the branches, the water
through the stones, the fire
in the hearth, the earth
underfoot.

Out at the water's edge, standing,
among the churchyard's yews, kneeling,
as the last sun of evening dies,
through graceless children dancing,
near the tide's full rip and ebb,
the moon's slightest sliver shining,
hands filled with grain, abundant —
every gift from the giver, given,
all three alive, made into a day.

WILLOW

Beneath its fan, a rare day of sunbreaks,
an afternoon alone, the fields and books
write themselves for once. I strain,
thinking of Christ in His desert. No rain?
To think the Lord our God saw months
of drought and in His thirst still wept.
To have the sun blanch you for weeks
and still find its warmth a blessing?

A man like that could wave his hand
and a crop of rye would turn to bread.
To think of such a man as could die
to show us all dying is always remade,
knotted through the soil's dark text
till at last we come again, green, anew,
pulled through the roots up into this
willow's gentle hair blowing, here, today.

If only you could see it! By God, look!
Out to sea a raft of shadow floats,
white spray catches brightly at its edge,
an unnamed brother gathers seaweed,
his robe wet in the surf, salt stains
like tree rings from days of such labor.
All at work, each a finger on the harp,
playing quiet as not to drown the voice.

Still, there are places we can never go,
deserts filled with a dry quiet so large
a stone falling down the valley wall
would rattle you with a fear He'd come.
You'd close the shutters for shade,
kick sand on the fire to cool the day.
Such silent places we'll never go, I know,
though through books I know them.

Rather we're blessed by cacophonies,
a lone blackbird pecking at the thatch,
the drip that follows, the night's sleep
that bends coldly round the puddle.
Next day, a monk stands on my shoulders,
skitters to fix it in a steady rain, smiling.
I'll admit, it's a constant struggle to love
the mud on my shoulders where he stood.

ASH

A man's made of threads,
his father and mother,
the sure knots, blood-red,
but his wider kin, too.

My uncle rose early,
sunrise yellow tied in,
dew on his boots,
the mud trail a wet yarn.

Washing at creekside
down from the dun,
where we swam, wading
in the water's cool weft.

The sun's cloud white,
rye thin near the byre,
the cattle lowing wove
days from my childhood.

Before now, but still,
old hands flit the shuttle –
as children they ran,
laid the trail before us.

Such is meaning made,
our lives laid across
the Weaver's beam,
thick as a giant's spear.

SECOND AICME

HAWTHORN

If the hand of God should hold me,
what blesséd thing would I do first?
By God, I'd light a fire to warm us,
tend the rye and sharpen the scythe,
string the beans, burn the weeds,
dip candles for the long days ahead,
scrape hides and fill pages with poems,
say a small kindness to Brother Aedh,
gather seaweed to rot winterlong,
stack stones in a wall-making prayer.

If the hand of God should hold me,
that day would look much like this day,
all of us rain-washed of grime and salt,
clean, cold and in need of warmth.
On that day, I will light a fire, I say
gently to old Brother Aedh as he sleeps –
then wander out to gather driftwood.
As always, in evening near the hearth,
when the fire's red strength wells up,
we open our hands and fill ourselves.

⊨
OAK

Walls. Miles of them, but no one for days
on these wind-whipped, landlocked lakes
we've been walking, looking for smoke or signs,
footprints, fish traps, a cared-for fence,
sheep scat or the moldy semblance of a crannog.
It's not as if they've run away; absence
is too full a word for these hills, Brother Maedoc
says after many quiet hours walking.

We pass the night in a blackened byre,
the first sign of men for days. At night, the fire
flitting in the fog barely breaks up the dark's
hard pieces, so we pray and both sleep, strong
in belief that we needn't be on guard here.
God is our sentry, I say, and we sleep well.
I wake in a drizzle, the sun's small circle
lighting the valley evenly in a grey haze.

Maedoc, alone and bent washing at creekside
turns to say the water's sweet as honey, and it is.
If the folk have long since left, at least
the place hasn't forgot to speak for itself.
We eat our turnips like apples as we walk.
The valley falls slowly below us, the byre
behind us, the full lay of Scotland before us,
we brace in the mud, trace verses in the wet

tangle of our arms, listen for a hint of talk
or the clap of horses, the rattle of chains,
a door slapped shut, a mother calling her son,
any human sound at all through the rain's din.
By noon the rain breaks and the cold comes.
We nearly turn back, quit speaking for miles,
till sitting silent by another long lake, a man,
his stark white body against the dark.

18

⊒ HOLLY

And near Bodmin Moor,
some years later it's said,
at great risk, such saying,
'The powers of nature
forgot their wonted courses,
and submitted to the will
of Saint Neot.' In great prose
this is written, but unwise.

You see, on angel's orders
he walked for weeks,
without bearing or trail,
stumbling in grace,
till in Cornwall, he knelt
with the hermit Gueryr,
and his servant came
with word a stream's pool
had filled with fish,
some three in number.

'Take but one each day,
and on the morrow
three there will always be.'
This the angel said.
He did so and stayed,
and lived well for years.

To take one was justice.
God, wearing a glove
called nature, brought
three and gave one.
It's so simple, you see.
What fools we'd be
to think men holy
who'd make nature
forget her course,
knowing whose hand
is wearing the glove.

⚏

HAZEL

I trust, as a child trusts his mother
to right his wrongs,
someone will write a story
that cleans the edges from my life.

A danger of history,
to purify the saints and mistake
Christ's forgiveness
for never having sinned.

I wish it weren't so,
for what grows in too-clean soil?
I'm assured by you, Bede, that none
of your flowers did.

To spare the reader these roots
is a failure to write
an umbilicus into the page,
to 'give what God has given.'

Bede, you told us no one's wiser
than him who ponders,
before going hence, what within
his soul will be judged at death.

Your death story says
you sat speaking John's book
in common tongue
to a scribe on a bright day.

You died with full flourish –
as the last words fell
from your mouth to his pen
you intuited a proper end.

The whole world would not,
you said, have room
for the books that would
be written. In Christ's name,

Amen.

APPLE

On the days the winds blow ill I enter them,
and on the days they lift the world, too –
the threshold, the naked green,
the ground and its seam,
the breath that passes in between,
across the bridge, then no bridge, just crossing,
through the night, then day without morning,
the harvest taken though never sown,
a docked ship, never on the horizon,
fruits in the market, no sign of the merchant –
the commerce of the breath.

On the days the rains flood the streams I swim,
and on the days they bless the fields, too –
to tread the cloying blue,
my thin body washed anew,
a held breath before bursting through,
to float in between, in a head of wind
with feet soaked cold, shoulders at the waterline,
a star suspended in a lake of night,
words floating on the water clock's surface,
a barrel of rain, the pull of the drain –
the commencement of water.

On the days the earth cracks in the field I weed,
and on the fertile days, too –
the hand on the shovel knows little of the hole,
to walk at night through the just-plowed field,
following furrows, feeling for stones,
to stumble, then fall, but not shout back –
a line of millions unlit in the quiet,
a well-trod trail, a late spring snow,
a wool-muffled cough on the edge of the field,
bareroots in the barrow, the maiden trees,
a grunt and thump but no warning called –
the commentary of the soil.

THIRD AICME

VINE

Weave the words into the world,
vines threaded through the trellis –
the cordon reaching out
like a brother's call across the field,
clusters and tendrils, the occasional spur –
the Father is the gardener.

This I saw in the garden: water,
water simply standing between rows.

Of course it came as rain,
and slowly filled the furrows all day.
I would call it a cold prophecy,
how the barley converses in it,
how our filled footprints in the field
bear witness to our walking.

This I saw in the garden
standing simply between rows.

In the silent ravel of its verses,
constrained, quiet and clean,
I rest on a rock and think of wine –
no grapes this far north –
though barley, barley treated rightly
gives something of the same.

IVY

To find himself Maughold set out
in white, into the white, with less than white thoughts,
his oarless, rudderless thick-skinned boat
cradled in the sea's open palm and sometimes fist
adrift for over a week before, in a hard sleep,
he woke wet where his boat scuttled
and sank a foot having found shore –
sentries of stones stood over him.

He'd hoped the thoughts would soften
in prayer and idle starless staring,
that his thoughts would get their bearing
as his will fell from him, as he drifted,
but that didn't happen. Instead he stuttered,
one thought in a hopeless loop,
of how he'd tried to put one over on Patrick.
The thinking of it went like this:

'To make the saint a fool, I wrapped
my friend Fáelán, still breathing,
hardly containing his laughter, in a shroud
and called Patrick to 'revive' him.
He came, placed his hands, and left.
With that, Fáelán was dead.
Connor sent our apologies to Patrick,
who came, shrove us, baptized us,
blessed dead Fáelán who then came to life,
and was given the water as well.
'Why not lead these men to kind acts
instead of foolery and drink?' He said.
So he set me in this boat alone,
for some seven days I've mulled this over.

'But the sand now underfoot shifts a bit,
I've made a fire and a boy brought me bread,
I'll build nothing but a shack,
sit long in the rain and watch the waves break,
and wonder what power this is
that washed me and swept me about
to land here, thinking on my faults,
on whether a man put to sea without a map
can arrive where he may be needed.'

⧻ BROOM

Philip's farmer knits the fourfold knot,
four threads: water, wind, earth and light.
The weighted plough and oxen pulling,
a stitch in the verse, the verse turned over,
countless knots to build the barley,
oats weave tight to choke the weeds,
a row or two of dyers broom,
then harvest and burning to set the seeds.

Take up the broom, but not to sweep,
learn from its flowers a fire-made newness,
burn the low brush from yourself and grow.

The wind and water's the quicker work,
the slower work earth and light,
these long rows of double seed stitches,
the farmer with his knitting pins,
Philip says, one pin for each thread.

Faith is the earth in which we take root,
hope the water through which we are nourished,
love the wind through which we aspire,
knowledge the light through which we ripen.
Use these tools that we may eat.

Also that we may know the sun-hewn dye,
for the Father is a farmer and a dyer both.
And this we know: true dyes soak through.
To be dyed in the light is to ripen,
to be born among meadowsweet,
oak flowers and not only broom,
to find a daily spring, a morning prayer,
the warm breeze that brings the new.

What God dips he dips in water,
and when you go to the pollen-blown river,
strip bare to your living human soil,
and clothe yourself.

ⵣ
BLACKTHORN

In this world you will have trouble,
You said, and so it is as You said –
Sick of mind am I,
apart from the others,
though we share a common table.

No prayer, no work, no laughter,
no counsel. No grip
on the feather when I pick up the pen.

I ask as they asked, Lord,
where have you gone?

I grieve of myself and know it foolish.
I know the cure but lack the herbs.

Give me drought, flood or famine,
let me help and know my place.
I'd willfully thirst with others,
carry them to higher ground,
wet a rag for their fever. But this

is a river without a ford,
a hard rain without a coat,
a pyre laid without a brand.

Take this, all of you, and eat of it –
I taste yeast failed to leaven,
a lack of salt, the black-burnt crust.
The wine ran out months back.

At the table with the others,
in the garden digging weeds,
at the podium near the window,
pen dipped in sloe gum I write.
I turn from you. *I* turn. I know.

ELDER

Though every seven years it's said
that west of westernmost Achill Head
an island appears in the fog.

Be it Uí Breasail or Tír Tairngire,
it's the latter I think on when I think of it,
for life lives always just there,
where the sun's nearly setting, doesn't it?

Were heaven not within, I'd hide it there –
when a farmer drinking milk on a break
breathes deep and shouts 'there it is!'
to his sons who shade their eyes to see,

or at the cliff a grieving widower stares
down at the sea's cold crashing below
and whispers in his hands 'here it is!'
what use to point to scripture and say

'No, you fools, it lies within –
Close your eyes and then you'll see
a land like this, though far less green.'

FOURTH AICME

✝
SILVER FIR

It's true the view from Iona
is scarce higher than at sea,
though from a rise on the island's west
I often see Malin Head at midday.

A vision more than a view.
Far off, to be sure, but no less clear.
And though prophecy's often
a fool's errand, I'll say what I've seen –

Out a window a woman stares
past the coast road's light traffic
over bayside trailers in Slievebawn
where rain drains to the sea.

Behind her, a clock, a calendar,
a rosary on the table.
Her son limps in a slicker outside,
swirling in the crown glass.

A small change day to day.
The water's slightly risen,
a few less cod than yesterday,
one fewer crake in the field.

And the oat field's failed.
Neither crake nor corax says much.
It's said fools only hear words,
only see named things. I see

far, but not far enough.
But fishers see beneath the keel,
what's ashore. She cracks the window,
holds her hand in the breeze.

There, amongst
Malin Head's whitewashed houses,
the wind is warming.
Have mercy on those who made it so.

‡
GORSE

When the sun's pulled fully into its flower
fall starts us gathering.
We bring the carts and fill the baskets,
stack bales in the fields and shoulder them home,
dig the holes and line their walls,
set the turnips in straw and cover.

The root cellar's the garden's dark mirror.
We work all night to put up carrots
in a tallow candle's light,
the fat from our cow who died of a sudden.
Milkless, we make the most of her.

In winter we'll cut her bones into buttons,
pack them in bags for trade.

When the boats come in spring
we'll learn in the bartering
how many buttons, cloth yards
and flour sacks a heifer's worth.

We'll gather a scattered horde
from the island's generous corners,
stack them on his decks,
and watch him nearly sink
for the weight of it all.
We'll buy the one with kindest eyes.

‡

HEATHER

I'd had a dream of endless rain.
In it I was sick with no mouth
to drink nor hands to wash.
That day I woke before dawn.

Thirsty, I stepped out in the fog,
cupped my hands in the spring,
lay on the stone marking its head
and nodded off. Rain fell

again, but as I stared into it,
it filled me, like the church of water
pouring from Morwenna's stone
into me, the sea that receives it.

I woke, this time at dawn.
Though I heard the morning
stirring, the shutting of doors,
the hollow wood of milk cans,

I stood a while in the water,
watched it fall down the stones
to the sea. So I followed,
and this is where it led me.

ASPEN

Whether he was Ce or a son
or grandson of Ce we couldn't say.
Clearly he was king. He fed us four
and after dinner his daughter,
or maybe his youngest wife,
sang of a long-dead ancestor's,
or war-dead brother's, ghost
that came as a wind to kill
the fields in fall, or perhaps
break the leaves from their stems.
He was outside, could we hear?
As she sang the women wept
and stared quiet before leaving
at song's end. No one spoke
until morning. This is their way,
we learned as weeks passed.

One day a band of men came,
blue spiral faces and arms,
ash spears, hair bones, shells
on strings, summer-bare feet,
a bag of fish, though mostly
they brought word. Word
we gathered by where they stared
and how hands mimicked
sowing and rowing and fear,
of harvests north, of portents,
of strange tides and storms,
of children born and dead,
old women and their illness,
broken bones and lost eyes,
the long walk west, the bare
rock that tore the raft apart,
and on and on till they shoved
bread in their bags and left
without farewell or thanks.

We hadn't spoken that day,
but Drostan nodded me to join
and we walked the river
to its fork, walked back
to find the others gutting
a deer, laughing at the smell,
how it hung cross eyed,
how it shat itself in fear,
a simple common ground.

The king's son some days later
took ill of a wind, they said,
or of the smoke of oak leaves,
or of birds flying east, or to sea,
or maybe it was us, and this
sent fear into me. Drostan,
calm, eyes near-closed warmed
his hands and placed them
on his throat and prayed.
This he did for three days.
We fetched water and herbs.
The boy woke at sunset,
the village sang for hours.

Days later, the king said
this river bend over here,
or this place west of the fire,
or this bank near the fish trap,
we couldn't tell which,
would make a fine homesite.
So we built a wood fence,
rose a wattle and daub,
slept sound the first night,
and next day all readied
to leave except Drostan
who stayed and prayed
as we went. The king said after

to his son in their tongue,
or at least it's said now he did,
that Drostan had prayed
'May the waves carry you,"
or 'Follow the setting sun,'
or 'Keep both feet forward.'

YEW

In the name of my father,
whose final story this is,
and of his son, myself,
whose pen sends this hence,
and of the spirit imbued in this page,
holding me to you, reading –
As it was in the beginning,
so too in the end –

In a small wind on a bright day,
having spent the morning
weeding and speaking little,
word arrived. Only a bindle
of words, and such a long way
they came. My father

was reading the harvest signs
when the Lord's voice
called from the earth
and he fell like a stone,
dead before the messenger
returned with the healer.

It was so before
but now there's no doubt
he's threaded through
every leaf and reed,
every stone in the stream,
every seed the world over
hums a thin song of him.

Watered and warmed,
the falling sun blesses him—
all living things on shore
and in the endless ocean
bear back and push forth,
an expression of him.

In this I have faith.

Though surely he's joined
a throng of souls forgotten,
their silt awash in the rivers,
fog sighed across marshes,
pushed from the valley floor
by God's shrugged shoulder
to the bare mountaintop
and swept up by a draft,
falling as rain on our faces
unaware we're drenched
in the cold spirit of them.

I have faith, too,
that to this I'll someday join –
And so I give thanks.

My father, I am not alone,
for you are with me,
now and well beyond the hour
of your death. I see it now,
as never before.
And may tomorrow
be as today.

Amen.

NOTES TO *THE BOOK OF TREES*

Below are notes to augment and compliment the poems. Each poem's title clearly comes from a particular ogham *fid*, and the poems are sequenced according to the four *aicmí* of the Tree Ogham, with each listed with the name of the tree in both English and Irish as well as the kenning ascribed

"SAINT COLUMBA'S PSALM"

This rendering of the poem, the only one in the sequence explicitly derived from an actual poem attributed to Columba, is incomplete, with the final stanzas missing. The final stanzas add an act of contrition to the poem, asking that he be forgiven and then adding (in a similar tone to those mentioned previously in the poem), to the litany of things that grace enables him to do in this remarkably "thin" place.

FIRST AICME (BEITH)

⊢
BIRCH (Irish: *beith*)
Beginnings, Renewal, Youth

1. "whose voice pulls seeds toward the light," see Isaiah 55:10-11.
2. "but this frigid day of Kentigern," Saint Kentigern, also known as Saint Mungo. Died 13 January, 614AD (feast day the same) in the Brittonic kingdom of Strathclyde (in modern day Scotland). Patron saint and founder of the city of Glasgow known for four main miracles: bringing a robin back to life after being killed by classmates in school, restarting a dead fire with a hazel branch, bringing a bell from Rome that was used to mourn the dead during funerals, and of ordering a messenger to catch a fish that had eaten the wedding ring of Queen Languoreth, who had been accused of adultery.

3. "Jerome's vulgar letters," St. Jerome, the translator of the original Latin vulgate Bible in 405 AD.

4. "Stone-hewn older shapes," the Irish ogham script, used to inscribe stones, predominantly with names as ownership markers, but also used as warnings and spells. The first use of the ogham in legend is by its legendary creator, Ogma mac Elathan, who wrote seven letter Bs on a birch in warning to Lug mac Elathan, meaning "Your wife will be sent seven times to the underworld unless the birch protects her." From that day the birch became the first letter of the ogham script, with L and F to follow. There are twenty standard ogham letters.

5. "It's right to refresh the memory," see 2 Peter 1:12-15

6. "Barrow, *bán,* Bangor, Bruden, etc.," In different traditions, the letters of the ogham are ascribed to various things as mnemonic devices. Thus there are (most prominently) the "Tree Ogham," (but also) the River Ogham, Color Ogham (*bán*= white in Irish Gaelic), the City Ogham, Fort Ogham, Virtue Ogham, Saint Ogham, etc., though the order of the letters is generally the same: B, L, F...

7. "like leaves across the earth's face..." see Revelation 22:1-3.

8. "At the river's edge let us begin," see John 7: 37-39 and Revelation 22: 2.

9. "as the trumpets blare," see Revelation 8-11.

ᚂ
ROWAN (Irish: *luis*)
Protection and control of senses

1. "I was a word in letters, a book in origin," is found in the "The Battle of the Trees," (*Cad Gaddeu* in Welsh) a poem preserved in the 14th century *Book of Taliesin*. The story of the poem follows primarily how the magician Gwydion brings the trees of the forest to life to fight as his army, but secondarily traces the birth of the flower maiden Blodeuwedd (see the notes for "Broom"). Made famous by Robert Graves in *The White Goddess* (where he incorrectly associates the trees with months), the quotation here comes from a translation, closer to

the Welsh, by Patrick K. Ford, whose *Mabinogi* many consider the definitive edition.

2. "Fursey's four fires," Saint Fursey (d. 650AD) , who received a vision of four fires burning in the air above a dark valley. Asking an angel what the four fires were, the angel replied that they were the four fires that would consume the world, and they were, respectively, the *falsehood* of living without fulfilling the promise of baptism, *covetousness* of worldly riches overly heavenly things, *discord*, when we needlessly offend others, and the *iniquity* of robbing and defrauding the weak. When the flames drew near Fursey, the angel exclaimed ""That which you did not kindle shall not burn you; for though this appears to be a terrible and great fire, yet it tries every man according to the merits of his works; for every man's concupiscence shall burn in the fire; for as every one burns in the body through unlawful pleasure, so when discharged of the body, he shall burn in the punishment which he has deserved."

3. "The army at Cúl Dreimhne," the Battle of Cúl Dreimhne, also known as the Battle of the Book, is where Columba instigated the Uí Néill clan to fight King Diarmait over the right to possess a copy of a psalter owned by Saint Finnian. The armies met at the foot of Benbulben Hill, where Diarmait, though a Christian, asked his druids to conjure a mist to envelop the Uí Néills. The battle caused nearly 3000 casualties and became a primary impetus for Columba's exile to Iona.

4. "We came to Iona," the island in the Inner Hebrides (in Columba's day a part of the kingdom of Dál Riata), where Columba took exile and founded a monastery.

≣
ALDER (Irish: *fern*)
Guidance

1. Saint Brigid of Kildare, lived c. 451-525. Her feast day is February 1, or Candlemas (which celebrates the presentation of Christ at the temple, the fourth joyful mystery of the Rosary) which is also the common day for the celebration of the pagan feast of Imbolc, the festival marking the beginning of spring,

the midway point between the winter solstice and the vernal equinox. The festival celebrates the fertile transition between the crone and the maiden (two aspects of the triadic Celtic lunar goddess tradition; the third being the mother).

WILLOW (Irish: *sail*)
Mystery, water-related subjects, feminine attributes, intuition

1. "Christ in His desert," see Matthew 4:1-11.

ASH (Irish: *nion*)
Ancient knowledge/wisdom, the weaver's beam

1. "the Weaver's beam," To raise a weaver's beam may have been a sign of peace in the Celtic world. The ogham letter ash, too, is thought by some to represent a five-pronged fork on a loom (or vice versa).
2. "thick as a giant's spear," see 1 Samuel 17: 7.

SECOND *AICME* (*HUATH*)

◅

HAWTHORN (Irish: *huath*)
Counseling, protection and cleansing

1.   "Burn the weeds," See Mark 13:24-30.

⊣

OAK (Irish: *duir*)
Strength and wisdom

1.   "till sitting silent by another long lake, a man," see Adamnan's *Life of Saint Columba*, Book 3, chapter 15.

⊟

HOLLY (Irish: *tinne*)
Justice and balance

1.   "Bodmin Moor," northeastern Cornwall, England.
2.   "'The powers of nature forgot their wonted courses…'" quote taken from *The Lives of the English Saints Volume 6*, by John Henry Newman (1903). Saint Neot, who lived at this site in Cornwall for a while with the hermit Saint Gueryr, is said to have been visited by Alfred the Great for counsel. The wellspring containing the fish in the story is near the current site of the Parish Church of Saint Neot in the Cornish town named after him.
3.   "God, wearing a glove/called nature," see Romans 1:20.

HAZEL (Irish: *coll*)
Wisdom and intuition

1. "Bede," b. 673 – 26 May 735, Doctor of the Church and, most famously, author of the Ecclesiastical History of the English People, though he wrote on the lives of the saints (notably for English history on Saint Cuthbert) and many theological, philosophical topics as well as anthologies of hymns, epigrams and other matters of poetry.
2. "to 'give what God has given,'" comes from Cuthbert's "Letter on the Death of Venerable Bede," which details the saint's final days and hours. Before dying, Bede sent a fellow monk to acquire what few belongings he owned ("pepper, napkins, incense") so that he could distribute them amongst his brothers, saying "The rich in this world are bent on giving gold and silver and other precious things; but I, in charity, will joyfully give my brothers what God has given unto me."
3. "no one's the wiser/than him who ponders..." is taken from the death song spoken by Bede on his last day.
4. "The whole world would not..." see John 21:25 in reference to the story, written by those present at the time of his death, that Bede was at work conveying the Book of John to a scribe. He finished the final lines of the manuscript and said later, as his final words, the Doxology, "Glory be to the Father..." See also Ecclesiastes 12: 11-12.

APPLE (Irish: quert)
The otherworld and choice

1. "On the days the winds blow ill..." See Ecclesiastes 11:5-6.
2. "On the days the rains flood," See Psalm 72: 5-7.
3. "a line of millions unlit," See Job 21: 33

THIRD AICME (*MUIN*)

⟍ VINE (Irish: *muin*)
Prophecy and inhibition or lack thereof

1. "Weave the words into the world/as vines threaded through the trellis," See John 15:4.
2. "The Father is the gardener." See Gospel According to Thomas, chapter 40: "Jesus said, 'A grapevine has been planted apart from the Father. Since it is not strong, it will be pulled up by its root and will perish.'" See also John 15:1.
3. "Constrained and clean," See John 15:2. In ancient Greek "he prunes" also means "he cleans."

⧧ IVY (Irish: *gort*)
Search for yourself and inner wisdom

1. Saint Maughold, d. 488. Arrived on the Isle of Man to become a hermit when Patrick sent him out in an oar-less coracle. This practice occurred in Ireland for several centuries after Christian conversion and was seen as a kind of endless pilgrimage, putting one's fate wholly in God's hands. It was often done as a form of penitence, a *peregrination pro Christo*, which had a "lesser" form, where the penitent did not leave the island, and a "superior" form, where the penitent left Ireland for good, which was referred to as "white martyrdom." For more on the "colors" of martyrdom (red, green and white), see the *Cambrai Homily*, the earliest known Old Irish homily, composed sometime between the 7th and 8th centuries.
2. "sentries of stones stood," the stone circle, a ring of Neolithic passage graves, at Meayll Hill on the Isle of Man.
3. "The thinking of it went like this:" The story that follows is a local legend still commonly told on the Isle of Man.

≢

BROOM (Irish: *ngetal*)
Working and tools

1. "Philip's farmer knits the fourfold knot," from the gnostic Gospel According to Philip: "Farming in the world requires the cooperation of four essential elements. A harvest is gathered into the barn only as a result of the natural action of water, earth, wind and light. God's farming likewise has four elements - faith, hope, love, and knowledge. Faith is our earth, that in which we take root. And hope is the water through which we are nourished. Love is the wind through which we grow. Knowledge, then, is the light through which we ripen."
2. "a row or two of dyer's broom," *genista tinctoria*, a plant common to Europe and traditionally used to make yellow dye.
3. "a fire-made newness," many kinds of broom are a "fire-climax" species, which are adapted to regular stand-replacing fires which kill the upper part of the plant and allow for regrowth from the roots.
4. "the Father is a farmer and a dyer both," again, from the gnostic Gospel According to Philip: "God is a dyer. As the good dyes, which are called 'true', dissolve with the things dyed in them, so it is with those whom God has dyed. Since his dyes are immortal, they become immortal by means of his colors. Now God dips what he dips in water."
5. "meadowsweet, oak flowers and...broom," In the *Mabinogi*, Blodeuwedd is a woman made (by the magicians Math and Gwydion) of broom, meadowsweet and oak flowers, created in order to wed Lleu Llaw Gyffes, who is under a taboo that he may not marry a human wife.

≢

BLACKTHORN (Irish: *straif*)
Trouble and negativity

1. "In this world you will have trouble," see John 16:33.

2. "sloe gum," the gum of the blackthorn (*prunus spinosa*) was used as an ingredient in ink during the Middle Ages in Europe.

≣

ELDER (Irish: *ruis*)
Entrance to the otherworld and the fair folk

1. "Uí Breasail," a phantom island that's said to appear surrounded in a mist in the Atlantic, west of Ireland on one day every seven years. The island, even when visible, cannot be reached.
2. "Tír Tairngire." As with the more commonly-known Tír na nÓg, the "Land of Youth" in Irish myth, Tír Tairngire is either a part of, or another name for, the Otherworld. The name in Old Irish means the "Promised Land," and it is sometimes believed to be underground, other times believed to be an island, where gods and ancestors are thought to live. Many stories speak of searching for it, but most notably Saint Brendan the Navigator, who, in his *Navigatio*, sets out on his journey to find it. Whether he discovered it, or America, remains to be answered.
3. "No, you fools, it lies within," see Luke 17: 20-21.

FOURTH AICME (*AILM*)

✚
SILVER FIR (Irish: *ailm*)
Far seeing and knowledge of the future

1. "A vision more than a view" See Columba's prophetic poem: "In Iona of my heart, Iona of my love/instead of monk's voices/shall be the lowing of cows;/but if the world shall come to an end/Iona shall be as it was."
2. "And though prophecy's often/a fool's errand," see Mark 6:4-6
3. "one fewer crake in the field," *crex crex*, a member of the rail family of birds that, while still abundant throughout Europe, has lost enormous numbers in recent years due to loss of habitat, early mowing of hayfields, and the proliferation of grasslands for other crops.
4. "neither crake nor corax," *corvus corax*, the common raven. See also, the 5th century BC founder of ancient Greek rhetoric, Corax of Syracuse, whose name means "crow" and who is best remembered as the person who invented the Doctrine of General Probability, which states that people are most likely to believe what they are already inclined to think is true.
5. "But fishers see beneath the keel,/what's ashore," see Revelation 18:17-18.

‡
GORSE (Irish: *onn*)
Collecting things to yourself

1. "fall starts us gathering," the common gorse, *ulex europaeus*, flowers in late autumn and through the winter.

HEATHER (Irish: *ur*)
Healing and homelands

1. "lay on the stone marking its head," Columba's grave on Iona is marked by a stone said to have been his pillow. See also Adamnan's *Life of Saint Columba*, Book 2, chapter IX.
2. "pouring from Morwenna's stone," Saint Morwenna, the patron saint of Morwenstow, Cornwall. Her name is thought to be a Welsh cognate of "maiden" (see note for "Broom" on Blodeuwedd as well as "Alder" note on St. Brigid), though in life she lived as a hermit on a high cliff before building a church nearby. She carried the church's stones on her head from the cliff and when she once stopped to rest, the site where she set the stone down poured forth with water, establishing a spring that runs to the west of the church to this day.

ASPEN (Irish: *edad*)
Communication

1. "Whether he was Ce…" A son of the legendary Pictish king Cruithne (whose name means "Pict"), Ce is said to have ruled in what is now Banff, Buchan and parts of Aberdeenshire. The region of Aberdeenshire is where Columba and Saint Drostan established a monastery at Deer, on the banks of the river Ugie
2. Saint Drostan, a disciple and close friend of Columba who was one of the twelve "brethren of Columba" who sailed to Scotland when Columba was exiled in 563AD. Columba traveled into Pictland with Drostan and left him behind at Deer to establish a monastery on land granted by a local Pictish chieftan whose son was saved from a virulent illness through prayer. Most of what we know of Drostan is from the famed *Book of Deer*, a 10th-12th century manuscript that contains the earliest surviving Gaelic writing from Scotland.

YEW (Irish: *idad*)
Death and rebirth

1. "It was so before/but now there's no doubt," see Psalm 88:9-12.
2. "In this I have faith," see Psalm 16:9-11.
3. "And so I give thanks," see Psalm 35: 18.

AFTERWORD

While most of the prior notes are self-explanatory, a few words should be said about the nature of the connections between Saint Columba, the druids of his day, and the ogham script with which they wrote. Likewise, it is worth mentioning the significance of how the letters of the ogham are conceptualized, how they themselves are arranged, and some of their uses.

COLUMBA AND THE DRUIDS OF HIS DAY

The name by which he is more commonly known in the English-speaking world, Columba, was the Latinized form of his name, derived from the Irish Gaelic "Columcille" meaning the "dove of the church." As with the ambiguity of his name, stretched between the ancient Irish world and the Latinate world of the Church, Columba's connections to the druids and the ogham script that they learned, used and taught are complicated. We know that beyond being baptized and mentored by his foster uncle, Saint Cruithneachán, he was also educated by members of the *fili*, the professional class of druids, and that he clearly held them in high esteem well beyond his childhood, even though he often had dramatic conflicts with them. Little is known of Columba's childhood, but it is worth considering some of the conflicts that he had later in his life as a way of gleaning the complexity of Columba's relationship with the druids of his day.

One such conflict occurred during the Battle at Cúl Dreimhne, often referred to as "The Battle of the Book." The battle itself was the culmination of an argument over the right to copy a psalter (that was in St. Finnian's possession) that left 3000 casualties and played a significant role in Columba's later exile to Iona. During the battle, King Diarmaid, though Christian, is said to have brought pagan druids who conjured a fog and caused much confusion. Interestingly, though Columba clearly would have taken offense at the indigenous magic used by the druids, in his "Lorica," a prayer of protection presumably written as Columba fled King Diarmaid to the mountains, he claims that his druid, his teacher, is Christ himself:

> I reverence not the voices of birds,
> Nor sneezing, nor any charm in the wide world,
> Nor a child of chance, nor a woman;
> My Druid is Christ, the Son of God.

It is not difficult to imagine that an Irish priest and scholar would conflate Christ's role as "rabbi" with the *fili* that he studied with and that he himself became. But clearly Columba's respect and tolerance had limits. Another story told in the *Life of Columcille* compiled by Manus O'Donnell in 1532 (translated by O'Kelleher and Schoepperle in 1918) tells the following story of Columba's arrival to Iona:

> On the even of Pentecost they cast anchor on that island; and there were druids there, and they came in the guise of bishops toward Columcille. And they said to him that it was not right for him to come on that island and that themselves had been there afore him sowing the Faith and piety, and it had no need of other holy men to bless it.

> 'It is not true what ye say,' saith Columcille, 'for ye be not bishops in truth, but druids of Hell that are against the Faith. Leave this island. Not to you hath God granted it.'

> And at the word of Columcille the druids left the island (201).

Whether Columba meant to differentiate between "druids of Heaven," who would embody a degree of Christian sympathy and "druids of Hell," who do not, we'll leave to another scholar to discern. Clearly, for all of the respect he accorded the *fili* who played a part in educating him, he didn't tolerate all of them. Adomnan's *Life of St. Columba* tells many other such stories, particularly those portraying tensions surrounding various kings and their druid advisors as Columba traveled and proselytized among the Picts.

Even through the complicated relationship Columba had with the *fili*, we can still assume that there were things that we can assume he would have learned from these *fili*. Of particular importance here, we can assume that he would have learned the ogham script, as learning the script was a hallmark of the druidic education. This assumption is not without scholarly evidence. In the introduction to his translation of the *Auraicept na n-Éces*, (the "Scholars' Primer"), a 7th century Irish grammatical text translated by George Calder in 1917, Calder claims that education under the *fili* included, from the first year on, an in-depth study of the ogham script, its uses and its literature (*xxi*). Columba would almost certainly have been educated under a similar curriculum as a child.

A FEW NOTES ON THE OGHAM SCRIPT

The ogham script is an alphabet used amongst the druids and known by many literate early Christian converts in 4th to 9th century Ireland. The primary text of ogham study, and the source for most of the information we know of the ogham during this period, is the *Auraicept na n-Éces*, though the book has since inspired many notable commentaries and has been greatly added to in its scope. There are many variations of the symbols of the alphabet themselves, and even more variation in the names of the letters and the ways they are remembered and compiled, so glossing the basic form and function of the script is difficult, though some general statements can be made.

The ogham traditionally has twenty letters, though other letters, referred to as the *forfeda*, were later added. The alphabet is arranged in four groups of five letters, with each letter called a *fid*, or "tree" in the Irish language. This idea of the letter as a tree takes on a deep resonance in later ogham studies, as I'll discuss below. Each group of five *feda* (plural of *fid*, "trees") are combined in an *aicme*, or "class." The *aicmí* are ordered according to the shape of the *feda* within it, and the staff that the *feda* are written may be vertical or horizontal). An angled bracket comes at the beginning and end of a phrase or sentence. Thus (with their Latin equivalents below them, we get):

The first *aicme*'s *feda* form with right- or downward-pointing *feda*.

B, L, F, S, N

The second with left- or upward-pointing *feda*.

H, D, T, C, Q

The third with diagonally-crossed *feda*.

M, G, NG, Z, R

The fourth with perpendicularly-crossed *feda*.

A, O, U, E, I

Notably, however, five more *forfeda* representing a series of vowels are often added as a fifth *aicme* alongside the traditional twenty *feda*, though these have less predictable shapes.

EA, OI, UI, IA, AE

With these basic *feda* shapes, the *Auraicept na n-Éces* gives the following passage to help remember the forms of the letters:

> These are their signs: right of stem, left of stem, athwart of stem, through stem, about stem. Thus is a tree climbed, to wit, treading on the root of the tree with thy right hand first and thy left after. Then with the stem, and against it, and through it and about it (71-2).

When written, the *feda* can be placed either vertically or horizontally in sequence, very often on a standing stone, though some of the ogham variants were designed exclusively for manuscript writing. Ellison points out, for example, that those with extensive loops or circles are likely intended only for manuscript composition (2). The letters themselves come in 122 known script varieties (though not all are found in the *Auraicept na n-Éces*), some more similar to the basic symbols shown above than others. The "Interwoven Thread Ogham," for example, uses roughly the same basic form (left/right/diagonal/horizontal) with 1-5 repeated lines, but doubled so that the lines of the letters weave together. The "Great Dotting Ogham," has dots instead of lines. And the "Place Ogham," boxes in the lines of the *feda*. Ellison notes that a student under a druid's tutelage was expected to fluently learn all 122 oghams in their first year of study.

COLUMBA AND THE OGHAM SCRIPT

The letters of the ogham had uses and connotations that went well beyond their practical use in marking territory and documenting hereditary succession. In no small part because the letters had such variety and were tied, through the mnemonic systems used to memorize them (which are discussed more below), to a wide range of objects, people and places, the letters were understood to have spiritual significance, poetic connotations, and magical uses.

As mentioned, Columba would have known the ogham script, but beyond his simple knowledge of the script, we can also make a few assumptions about his deeper knowledge of the script's other significant features. We know, for example, from several ancient sources that Columba advocated or the commitment of the druidic wisdom traditions into writing, particularly their poetry. It would seem to follow that he would likely have known and appreciated in particular the poetic and spiritual significance ascribed to each letter of the ogham described in the *Auraicept na n-Éces*, which was written within a couple generations of his death.

With a sound knowledge of the *feda* and the other ogham variants, Columba would have also been aware of the various mnemonic systems developed to help students memorize the letters. These mnemonic systems are complex and this complexity plays no small role in how the letters have come to take on deeper, resonant spiritual significance over time. The *Auraicept na n-Éces* comments on the way that a student may be measured not only in memorizing their names, but also by recognizing the various rhetorical and grammatical powers, strengths and weaknesses of each *fid*. It states:

> What is measured with regard to Ogham letter? Not hard. That thou mayest know their number and their singleness, their size and their smallness, their power and their want of power, their strength and their weakness (71).

The latter phrases, "their power and their want of power, their strength and their weakness" implies that the letters themselves were charged with a kind of energy and that each letter offers a different kind and degree of energy in their use. This is not so different in ways to any other symbol system, but the way it is discussed has much in common with a magical worldview akin to that discussed in William Covino's 1994 book *Rhetoric, Magic, and Literacy* and discussed in depth by many other notable scholars.

THE OGHAM SCRIPT'S WIDE VARIETIES

The different types of ogham may have differing *feda* or other symbols, but this variety is largely in its visual aspect; most oghams ascribe a similar phonetic value to a given letter within a given *aicme*. We know this because in all of the mnemonic systems, the "name" of the letter begins with the sound (in Irish) that the letter phonetically represents. Thus we have over 122 different written letter systems, and then we have a separate tradition of letter names to ascribe a phonic value to the letters within each. The phonic names can thus be ascribed to any variations of the script, be it the "Great Dotting" or the "Interwoven Thread," or any of the other of the 122 variants. These lists of scripts and phonic names are often inconsistent, and thus knowing how each letter was exactly treated in Columba's day is impossible at times, but enough consistency exists that some conclusions can be drawn.

One aspect that is particularly confusing is that some of the scripts have the same name as a mnemonic system. The "Tree Ogham," for example, which is the most common ogham, is both a naming system and a script. But there are many other mnemonic naming systems, as well, such as the "Bird Ogham," the "Saint Ogham," "Color Ogham," "River Pool Ogham," etc. which all use roughly the same letter symbols, but have different names for them. A correlate would be to consider that in English the letter "h" is pronounced "aetch," but in German is "ha." So in the Tree Ogham, for example, the first letter ⊢ ("B") is "beith," (or Irish for, coincidentally, "birch"), but in the River Pool Ogham it is "Barrow," a river in Ireland. Each letter is thus ascribed a name so that the list of the letters can be remembered as a list of place names, animals, churches or other significant things that can foster better memory and also serve the ulterior purpose of implying a new register of meaning.

To make things even more complicated (but also more meaningful), each letter, beyond having a name and a symbol, is ascribed a particular kenning that augments the meaning of the name. These phrases are collected in a text called a *bríatharogam*, which is essentially a list of the letters and the kennings that accompanies each. According to McManus, three *bríatharogaim*, or anthologies of such kennings, have been preserved, and each lists variants on the kennings. We find in these three *bríatharogaim* an inconsistency where many of the letters are not given the names of trees, but rather other qualities. The symbol ⊣ (H) for example, named *huath*, is implied to mean in the three *bríatharogaim* something akin to "fear" and is given the kennings "a pack of dogs is *huath*," "blanching of faces," and "most difficult at night." But the *Auraicept na n-Éces* glosses *huath* as "hawthorn," and gives the kenning "because it is formidable for its thorns." The most popular reading of these kennings, and the preeminent mnemonic system, the Tree Ogham, comes not from these three *bríatharogaim*, but through the glosses of each letter found in the *Auraicept na n-Éces*. Why the version given in the *Auraicept na n-Éces* is the most popular is still a matter of debate, though it is not difficult to imagine that much of this popularity comes from a desire to see all the symbols, names and kennings as all being "of a kind," namely all tree-related, thus rendering them more readily coherent and comprehensible.

The evidence of the *Auraicept na n-Éces* and elsewhere indicates that the druids of ancient Ireland were versed in the nearly endless permutations of the ogham, but we may be able to conjecture that the Tree Ogham is likely the one most familiar to Columba, as again the composition of the *Auraicept na n-Éces* was completed not long after his death and would likely have chronicled a common reading of the *feda* circulating at the time.

OGHAM AND THE RELIGIOUS IMAGINATION

Most scholars and modern writers point to Robert Graves' book *The White Goddess* as the primary source for the Tree Ogham's popularity. Borrowing and changing ideas from ogham scholar R.A.S Macalister's *The Secret Languages of Ireland* and other sources (such as Roderick O'Flaherty's *Ogygia*) where he deemed fit, Graves manipulated the character, and sometimes even the names, of the ogham letters to fit his new mythical vision of the script. In the book, Graves develops a "tree calendar" and claims that the magical characteristics of the calendar come to us from the druid Taliesin (made famous in the King Arthur stories, though his fame as a poet in Wales pre-dates those stories). Whether popular culture co-opted these easier, and more consistent, glosses of the kennings because of Robert Graves' later invention of this poetically salient "tree calendar" based on the tree kennings, or whether popular culture has co-opted this "tree ogham" simply because the more easily-glossed kennings of the *Auraicept na n-Éces* make for a more coherent system will remain up for discussion. The scholarly authority of Graves' book is dubious at best, but it has produced a tremendous amount of subsequent literature, both in poetical works and in commentaries on the efficaciousness and mythic power of his text. Suffice to say that the impact that the Tree Ogham has had on the modern religious imagination is evident to anyone who spends a few hours researching Celtic lore and the ogham script.

While Graves' work is not a reliable scholarly source for the ogham's use in spiritual practice, there are a few ancient sources providing some precedence for the script being used as a tool for divination and spiritual exercise. Ellison points out that one of the "other oghams," the "Boy Ogham," was used specifically for the divination of a child's sex before birth. He also details research (from the McManus book *A Guide to Ogham*) where a passage found in the *Tochmarc Étaíne* ("The Wooing of Etain"), an early text in the Irish mythological cycle, speaks of a druid being tasked with finding Etain, who has been missing for a year, and he uses yew rods inscribed with ogham letters to perform this task. Ellison also alludes to a reference to the use of rune staves in Tacitus' *Germania*, where the tribes of Germany in the first century CE were said to have used "rods of nut-bearing wood" to divine, and these may well have been ogham staves, as well. Surely there were residual Celtic practices like these all over pagan Europe, though they would have been most explicitly tied to the Celtic mythos in Ireland and Britain where the language and culture of the Celts remained most intact and untouched by Roman and Germanic influence.

Beyond Graves, there has been much literature focused on recovering the pagan spiritual practices that may be imbedded in the ogham, and there has been much literature about Columba and the earthy, nature-focused Christianity he seems to have practiced. What has heretofore been lacking in the literature is a bridge between the pagan spiritual practices that Columba would have been well-versed in as a student, and the spiritual practices of Christianity that came to dominate his worldview. Given Columba's proximity to the composition of the *Auraicept na n-Éces* both in terms of time and place, it seems fair to think that he would have known of the book, or at the very least its content. It would likely follow too that he would have known the ways that the names and kennings implied spiritual significance to each *feda* and how that significance played out in spiritual and magical practice in his day. Even with Columba's presumed Christian orthodoxy, by the simple fact of his linguistic and cultural heritage there would have been an inevitable melding of spiritual practice between the pagan Celtic world and the Christian, especially so soon after the Christianization of Ireland.

Much of the literature on what's commonly referred to as "Celtic Christianity" today focuses on these blended traditions while hewing to the essential core of Christian teachings. It should be noted too, that except in the most orthodox or fundamentalist circles, this discussion is not seen as heretical, but rather a vital means of exploring Christian practice and prayer.

THE INVISIBLE VIOLENCE OF CHRISTIAN-CELTIC ECUMENISM

In the seemingly innocuous way that people erect Christmas trees in church, color eggs at Easter, and make sugar skulls for All Souls Day, it is easy to believe that the melding of Christianity with indigenous culture and tradition has everywhere been an open dialog that took place over a long time and is, accordingly, "organic" in its current forms. In thinking of these traditions, we tend to flippantly note that they all draw from a deep, old pre-Christian past and are now expressions of some remote conversation that took place in a mythic past that was as equitable as it was loving. These traditions in this way seem to have come about without any sense of contradiction. But our flippancy typically skews the politics of how this "conversation" has unfolded. We only have to look to Theodosius, Harold Bluetooth and Charlemagne for some particularly bloody examples. The talk of "Celtic Christianity" is particularly guilty of this, drawing on stories of the nearly bloodless conversion of Ireland and Britain as a mythic source of the organic melding of cultures and religions and other such claims of inviolate conversion to Christianity. But this privileged and blindfolded view of this historic moment fails to see other forms of cultural and epistemological violence that unfolded in the Ireland of Columba's day.

As a corrective, we must admit that while the stories of the medieval Irish, Welsh and Britons who set out to become "white" and "green" martyrs (who pushed out to sea in coracles or walked deep into the wilderness to put their absolute faith in God) because there were no actual "red" martyrs made during the conversion of the island, are intriguing, the idea that Ireland's conversion to Christianity was "bloodless" fails to see those who lost their lives and/or livelihoods *opposing* Christianity's spread. This is to say nothing of the violence perpetrated against the lifeways, collective memory and rituals of those living through the transition. The loss of the orally-transmitted knowledge of the druids is only one easily-seen example of this. It is commonly held in some circles, for example, (though these claims don't seem to hold up under scholarly scrutiny), that the "snakes" that Patrick expelled from Ireland were not serpents (which Ireland seems to have never had in the first place), but rather the druids, whose arm tattoos made them into the easy metaphor of snakes in the stories of subsequent centuries. Whether or not this history is true (as Isaac Bonewits and others have worked to promote), the reality was surely that many druids and their followers faced incredible scrutiny and surely sometimes physical violence with the advent of Christianity in Ireland. Here, however, we may again find a viable (and vital) bridge by considering Columba's unique place within this history. This is not to erase that violence, but to find a way to recover the energy of that violence and write it into the body of "Celtic Christian" literature to avoid any "purification" that could take place otherwise.

ANCIENT ECUMENISM IN THE MODERN WORLD

The degree to which Columba himself participated in the preservation of the druidic oral tradition into a body of written work remains somewhat in question, though Columba seems to have had some hand in that transition. Richard Sharp documents how, in an account written years after Columba's death (in a preface added by Ferdomnach, abbot of Kells, in the early 11th century to the *Amra Coluimb Chille*), the claim is made that Columba had attended the convention at Druim Cett in 575AD in order to intercede on the part of the druid poets who faced banishment at that time. Similarly, it is hypothesized by Daniel P. McCarthy that Columba himself oversaw, but may have even himself written, some of the earliest material of the *Annals of Ireland*, which was composed at Iona during Columba's years as abbot. This material was presumably at least in part a transcription of works from the druidic tradition that had theretofore only been transmitted orally. Steeped in the learning gotten from his druid teachers and a native of the culture they played a significant role in maintaining, Columba, we can assume, would have had an ecumenical worldview when it came to the indigenous culture and tradition of his native country. The violence he would have inevitably been a part of doesn't change his import in this transition. But his worldview is less the point than the fact that *he lived through the transition*. We are often guilty of trying to reconstruct past worldviews as a way to recover something, some ecological or social morality, that's been lost. This never works because the world has moved on, even if we fail to understand how it has done so.

This doesn't mean that there is no value in thinking of some earlier worldview, it is only to claim that its recovery is impossible. To feel the deepest possible resonance of Columba's ecumenical worldview, it may require remembering that the Greek root of the word "ecumenical" comes from *oikoumenikos*: "belonging to the inhabited earth," and that the earth in this sense is continually inhabited. The earthy, grounded spirit and prose of Columba's writings and hagiography, growing as they surely did from a tapestry woven of pagan and Christian mythos and culture, can serve a similar ecumenical purpose today, as long as we aren't anachronistic in our motives. We must remember that much has been written of Columba, the ancient Ireland he lived in, the history of Iona as a pilgrimage site, etc., and unless this is intended to give us ritual and experiential access to that history, it is not enough. We would be wise to remember that his was a dangerous and brutal world, even for a "man of God." Lives were short and constantly under threat of starvation, slavery, war and the elements. It was a world that had just turned the corner after a collapse; Rome had fallen a mere hundred years before. Lives came and went like the seasons and most were only remembered by the soil and in the threads of stories in the places where they left their mark. We must respond to the violence from then that we can still feel playing itself out around us (in the world and texts we live with). We must, in other words, work *through* that violence in light of the mythic memory of Columba and his worldview. In our hyperextended modern world, admitting and working through this violence becomes a way of flourishing creatively, spiritually and vitally in the midst of the very likely social and ecological calamities we face. As always, there is no way out but through.

It is under these presumptions and in this spirit that these poems are written.

WORKS CITED

Calder, George. *Auraicept Na N-éces; the Scholars' Primer*. Edinburgh: John Grant, 1917.

Ellison, Robert L., Rev. *Ogham: The Secret Language of the Druids*. Tucson, AZ: ADF Publishing, 2007.

Graves, Robert. *The White Goddess: A Historical Grammar of Poetic Myth*. New York: Farrar, Straus and Giroux, 1966

McCarthy, Daniel P. "The Chronology of the Irish Annals." *Proceedings of the Royal Irish Academy*. Vol. 98C, No. 6, 1998, pp. 203–55.

McManus, Damian. "Irish Letter-names and their Kennings." *Ériu* 39, 1988, pp. 127-168.

O'Donnell, Manus. Betha Coluimb Chille, *Life of Columcille*. Trans. O'Kelleher & Schoepperle. Urbana, Illinois: University of Illinois Press, 1918.

Sharpe, Richard. "Druim Cett." *The Oxford Companion to Irish History* (Online Edition). Oxford University Press, 2007.

ACKNOWLEDGEMENTS

I would like to thank the following people, without whom this book would have been impossible.

My mother, Phyllis Conrey, for her continued love and support. Brigid Dunn, David McCallum, Lou Sogliuzzo, and my fellow Contemplative Leaders in Action at Le Moyne College: Gaven Ehrlich, Katie Finn, Karen Grella, Monica Merante, Katie Scanlon, Pat Shandorf, all of whom helped assure that these poems had purpose. Dana Driscoll, whose vision of the violence that marked the advent of the Christian era in Ireland provided the onus for this project. Kevin McKelvey, whose edits were invaluable. Emily Bender Murphy, whose brilliant art and kindness continue to inspire. The editors of *The Wayfarer*, who published the poems "Ivy" and "Willow," which appear in this book. Barbara Lawhorn, Lesha Shaver, Geof Carter, Nada Fadda, Jesse Nissim, Patrick Williams, Dana Olwan, and Ghassan Zeineddine for their words, wisdom and friendship. Jennifer Glancy, Phil Memmer, Maurice Manning, and Philip Metres for their generosity and time. Ron Starbuck, whose patience and trust allowed this book to take shape. And lastly Carol Fadda, who keeps us rooted wherever we go.